PLAYFUL VERSES II

PART I

MAANSHA @
MADHUVANTHI BASKARAN

"To the reason for my existence"

Contents

1. Make your way – Make it your way

Is it my turn
Can I do it?
Or better I quit.
Am I capable
To lead the road?
Enough with the questions
Now, get on the board.
Sail through the storm
Rebel compelled norm
Make it your way
Save your words
It's not the last day
So just stay
And finish the race
You've got backup of you.
Even if you tiptoed
You can make a new road
It can't be a dead end
You will be your best friend.

2. Hoping for a change

Denial is hopeless
It's fated to feel it
Thoughts of negativeness
Isolate and seal it
Forever, chained to the loop
You'll never find the way out

It's all about
Standing the pain, without gain,
Still hoping for a change.

Wandering over a pendulated hope
You're stronger to deny
The loop away
Just untie the rope
And live your day
You've still got a long way
Roll over the dirt
You may get hurt
Step down and step up
Play along, but don't get stuck
Stop hoping and be the change.

3. I'm sleepy

I wish time can hurry
My vision turned blurry
The clock is ticking lazy
Can't control feeling dizzy
Spiked with lethargy
Drained, no energy
I find me pinching myself
I see it is of no help
Can't hear the alarm beep
Black out, now I'm asleep.

4. You

This possesive feel is killing me
Someone true to heart is hard to see
True colours unveil, when you look beneath
Tormenting words, make it hard to breathe.
I often get mad at you
Grab my phone, to question few
I'm left with no choice,
When I hear your voice,
I lower my tone
Instantly, reason still unkown.

5. My tag along

Flare up moody mind
You're no longer weak
Time to show up
Stop the hide and seek
Those usual chores
Are no longer yours
Anything, everything
Will now on be your thing
Days shedding tears
Looked down by my peers
Not anymore
It's time to score
Back to swag
The loneliness tag along.

6. Forgiving Flora

Dear varied green
Only you can clean
The mess we've left
It's solely human theft
We think there's no need
To plant the right seed
Waiting the disaster
To harm our latter.
I hope we can be forgiven
And not be driven.

7. Never retire

Sick memories,
Only stop the victories
Change your enemies,
So you don't stag as frenemies.
Enjoy all you could before you're twenty,
Cause, when you pass it, you can't be.
But, still, you can ...
Set the stage on fire
It's never late to desire
And it's not yet time to retire.
Just keep on going higher.

8. Alone on a rainy day

Trees are you singing for me
Breeze are you swinging those trees
Pitter patter music by the cloud
I hear the thunder growling out aloud
Chilly nights giving all the warmth I need
All I need was you all this time indeed
I can find you everywhere and everytime
You reach out to me like a baby of mine
You never leave me alone
But I didn't notice it, for which I atone.

9. Trick or Treat

Trick or Treat
I know it's too late to retreat
Our fate is set to repeat.
I think of days that were sweet
But it was all plot for plan
Battle is, beyond the clan
Rising into power
The poor preyed, they devour
The money lenders coward,
Yet they make them suffer.
Now and all is never
So give up and move on
Making the battle empty
Can only lead life happy.

Playful Verses

To be continued..